Copyright © Jaune 2022
All rights reserved.

Fool's Gold

JAUNE

FOR YOU, MOTHER
I WILL LIVE
EVEN IF I WANT TO DIE
LIVE TO MAKE YOU PROUD
UNTIL I SEE YOU AGAIN

Contents

The Trenches 0

The Storm 51

The Forest 101

The Sunlight 147

CHAPTER I

THE TRENCHES

Open my mouth and pull out my tongue

No more words to be said

You own my voice, my body and soul

A marionette attached to your strings

I curl up my body and surrender to your control

If I plead and beg for freedom it means nothing to you

My voice in a box, tucked away like soft blankets

It echoes in the distance

It rings in my ears

No more talking or screaming

I shall learn in the silence

I have done my dance and the show is over

Slowly crawl to the door

Shape a key from my index finger

Grinding bone with rocks that you once threw at me

I hear your footsteps not far behind

I close my eyes and drift away

In this dreary dream I've built in my head

One where I unlock the door and leave this pain for dead

The Red Door

Open the door
Like you did before
Like you will again
Because you're weak
A frail being
No backbone
Forgive him
And restart the timer
Reset the anger
It will implode
One day is good
Maybe even two
But soon your anger will bubble
Overflow
Spill onto that hot burner
Causing smoke to rise
And tears to shed
Crawling on your hands and knees
Trying not to suffocate
Reaching oxygen is foreign
And when you do it's terrifying
The air is clean
And your flesh isn't burning
It almost feels wrong
Being safe

Familiarity is comfortable
Once the fire is out
To go back into that house
Wait for him to set the match
Burn into the hardwood
Turn to ash

He Is Fire And I Am Gasoline

Into that pit of despair
Into the void
That's embedded a hole inside your chest
No amount of happiness can fill
Broken
Like an old toy once played with
But now discarded
Forgotten
Just like that toy and so many other things
Brain melting into fire
Days blur, making me question my sanity
Losing time
Never having enough
You never did to begin with
Accomplish little things
But never satisfied
Taking steps but always feeling like you never move
Forever clinging to the easy route
Trying
Changing little by little
But the hurt is the same
Voices echo
Bouncing off the walls of your fragile skull
Living in your head just so you have a home
A safe place away from danger

Away from judgment and misdiagnosis
Where I don't have to be afraid
But is it safe?
Is anything safe?

Mental

We're heading in a downward spiral
And you don't seem to mind
Trapped in twists and turns
The end to this, I'd kill to find
Why do you like to torture me?
Or is it me that's hurting you?
We've lost all sense of being one
But you'll never see the truth

Toxic

I have never wanted anything in my life

Not as much as I want to die

Scour the earth for a purpose

And always end empty handed

I've felt this way for years

Yet no one sees me

Like, actually sees me

All I've ever wanted was a feeling

Comfortability, is it?

Or just simple, good old fashioned belonging

I fear I'll never understand

How can I keep going?

Taking steps I never thought I'd take

Blowing out birthday candles I never thought I'd see

Just searching for something

Anything to fill this emptiness

Episodes

So lonely
And I can't breathe
Face is numb
Legs are tingly
Feel like I'm dying
Palms are sweating
Am I broken?
Always wanted
To be normal
So sensitive
To every feeling
So intense
The pain always fleeting
Wrists bleeding
Turn your blind eyes
While I gasp for air
Always acting
Like you care

Traumatic

I shrunk myself
Down so small
I couldn't stop your foot from crushing me
Screaming so loud
Not a soul would hear me
Make a home in the floorboards
Befriend the dust that fills my lungs
Forgotten
And for what?
So you could stand tall?
To make you happy?
While I lay in misery
I thought you deserved better
Better than me
More than I could give
I had it backwards
If only I had seen
Before it was too late

Dust Bunny

You got me tripping
Over my own boundaries
Like skip rope
Unforgiving
Tosses me over and under
In the distance there's singing
Words I should know
I should have memorized
Every lie
"I love you" was the first
And still to this day
You throw it around as if you mean it
While on the ground I lay

Pavement

My problem

Used to be that I cared too much

About everyone

And everything

All the time

Now my problem

Is that I don't care enough

About anyone

Or anything

Numb

People break you until there's nothing left
Until those pieces turn to dust
Till you can no longer love

Dustpan

All I ever wanted

Was for you to feel what I felt

To love the way I love

To give what I gave

And all I ever got was empty hands

Reaching out

Clinging to any bit of intimacy you could show

Even if it wasn't a fraction of what I gave

I'd call it good enough

Because I loved you so

I gave all of myself

And got nothing

Warmhearted

Hatred is what fuels me

Every day I open my eyes

Angry

Ready to explode

But I don't

I repress

I go on

I do what needs to be done

Cater to everyone but myself

Hold back the tears I long to shed

The fire burns

In my belly, in my heart

It keeps me alive

When I want to give in

Want to just lay in the dirt

But I feel the heat

Let it consume me

Let it take control

Volcano

I've been suffocating in you
Draped in your blood stained linen
Breathing toxic fumes through the vents
Clawing at blank white walls till my finger nails break
For too long I've made excuses
Stood by your irrational choices
Let you silence my own
I've laid in defeat for years
On a floor, cold and dusty
The same floor you beat me into
With words like daggers that pierce my soul
Breaking me into pieces until I'm malleable
You shape me into who you want me to be
I follow your lead and let you destroy me
Nowhere to run in these four walls
A prison I signed in my blood
A place I once thought could be a home
There is no home for me
Not as long as you sit on your throne

King Of Nothing

Far and wide I have searched for a place to call my home
I roamed in forests and paced through deserts
Not a place to be seen that could contain me
I swam the ocean and journeyed below the deep
Dug through dirt and explored caves of dark and webs
I never give up searching
For a home made just for me
A place I belong, one where I don't have to pretend
Does such a place exist?
Even if not
I'll keep searching till I find it

There's No Place Like Home

She's not real
But a figment of my imagination
Forever still
With an anchor around her ankle
Weighing me down
Taking control
Slipping through my cracks
Darkness whispers foul
I tell myself to let go
"You don't have to be her"
But she lingers
Spreading through my veins
Sabotaging my every move

Depression

I feel dead

My body doesn't want to move

Mind is still

Breath cannot escape me

Stuck in place

Underground

The same mundane day

Playing over and over

As if I'm not even living

Just rotting away

Corpse

I wished upon a star
Last night, as I gazed out our window
That I could change you
That I could make you who you were
When we fell in love
But wishes
They're just a dream
Something you hope with all your might
Something you believe just may work
That it can be possible
I wished with every fiber of my being
That I could bring back the man
Who stole my heart with one gaze
But just like that star
That man is a lifetime away
And he burnt up in the sky long ago

Wishes

I know I'm stronger than this
Than this anger dwelling
The tears I hold back
The words I want to shout from rooftops
I know I'm better than this
And yet I'm still stranded
Helpless, alone
On an island made from my regrets
Slowly sinking into untamed waters
Letting it pull me under

Fight The Current

You ripped me from my roots
From out of the ground I was so fond of
I gladly obliged
Bowed to you as if you were above me
Altered my appearance
Abandoned my home
Left those I loved in the dust
Let my favourite songs go unheard
As If I could sweep who I was under a rug
As if you deserved all of that praise
Like who I was, wasn't good enough
I sat there fueling your fire
While you burned me away
I turned to ash and flew into the wind
Just so you would love me more
But you never loved me to begin with
You just loved my obedience

Gaslit

I try my hardest not to break
When I'm on the verge of exploding
Bury it within the layers of skin
Seal it away with a wax stamp
And yet it lingers
A feeling of uncertainty
A skip in my heartbeat
Loss of breath
It creeps in at the worst of times
When I think I'm finally free
Guard down and hopes high
I always end up sinking
No matter how high I get
My hardest is never enough

Losing Control

I am in control of me
And of whom I allow my company
So why am I down so deep?
With you drowning next to me
The sand is cold
In between our toes
Your skeletal hands hold me close
I'm locked in it seems, you'll never let go
As the water fills my lungs
I pray to escape
I scream but no one can hear
At the bottom of this lake
Claw at your bones that are squeezing me still
Nothing works
No release, no will

Swim To The Surface

Drowning in air
Trembling shakes
Making hearts palpitate
Deep breaths in paper bags
Try not to hyperventilate
Constant fear and self hate
Is this state of being the only way?
My own mind, I cannot escape
Clawing at the walls inside my brain

Anxiety

Your leash around my neck keeps you in power
The collar made of bones bruises my skin
Delicate black and blue like my heart
Lay defeated at your feet
I am yours to do your bidding
Pay me off like I'm your property
Chain me to the ground so I can't escape
I am your dog

Bitch

"Who are you?" She said

Looking into a cracked mirror

Your eyes are black

Lacking sleep

Your smile fades more with every day

Who are you?

The sparkle in your eyes has disappeared

Your hair remains uncolored

All the things you once loved lay dormant in a corner

You let yourself go

Wither away like autumn leaves

All your empty canvases haunt you in your dreams

Who are you?

Your voice has lost it's soul

Shoulders slouch and muscles weaken

When was the last time you sang?

When was the last time you've eaten?

Self destruction is dangerous

A game you no longer fear

You've lost yourself in this cage

Can't even enjoy the music

Can you even hear?

Who are you?

A shell of what you once were

Trapped inside looking out the keyhole

Deep down I know you're in there
The person you know you are
You just have to regain control
Who are you?
Looking back at me, you're not me
You're a stranger
I hope to meet you and know your face
I hope to see you smile again
For your eyes to glow
Your hair to blow in the wind on a sunny day
Come back to me
Through the cracks in the glass
So we can be one

BPD

Have you ever felt so trapped in darkness it becomes you?
Enveloping you in a cold embrace
It starts to feel like home
You could almost settle into its nest
Let it feed you scraps and call you it's own

You become someone else
Naive, fragmented
Someone you don't recognize
Someone fueled by one sided love and empty promises

You long to be who you once were
The days you basked in the sun haunt you
A faint memory of the better

You dream of paradise even when you're awake
Only to be grasping for false hopes that vanish the second your eyes open
You lay in defeat succumbing to the dark

Have you ever felt so trapped
You forgot your own name?
You forgot the taste of your favourite meal
The smell of flowers in may
You don't remember the last time you smiled genuinely

You've settled too far into the nest
Can you be free?

Have you ever felt so trapped
You're afraid to open your eyes?
Afraid to open your mouth
To let your voice be heard
Walking on eggshells is the custom now
It's just who you are
And you can never find anything better

Have you ever felt so trapped
Even your own heart doesn't believe you?
You plan to escape but you're dragged back

Into the darkness
In the envelope
Locked away in a desk drawer
Never to be seen by anyone
Faint whispers give you strength
But can you hear them?
Are you even listening?

Have you ever felt so trapped
You've lost all sense now
All sense of who you were

So weak and fragile
Like an infant left on a doorstep
Crying out for anyone to hold you
The one who had you has left you damaged

Can you grow to be better?
Will you rise from your bed with purpose?
Or stay tangled in the sheets
The only place you can feel safe for a moment
Take deep breaths and hope for the best

Have you ever felt so trapped
That even when the door is open you don't want to leave?
Brainwashed, manipulated
You no longer have control
What is real and what is fiction?

"I am nothing"
That is what you're told everyday
Not by the dark but by yourself
You chose this
You continue to choose the dark over the light
And you are still nothing, tangled in the sheets
In this bed made of dirt
In this grave you have dug

Have you ever felt so trapped
The devil's voice soothes you?
Even when you want to scream

When you want you run away
But he is the air you breathe
The hand that fed you in that nest
He embraced you when he could have picked anyone else

He lays those eggshells down just for you
Is that not enough?
How can you be so greedy?

Have you ever felt so trapped
You let the devil have his way so you can live in silence
You let him have you when all you want is sleep
To dream of paradise
Close your eyes and imagine anyone else has their arm around you
Anything to feel something other than pain

But can you ever open your heart to anyone but the devil?
Can you let the light in after living in darkness for so many years?
Will you rise with purpose or will you stay entwined?
The choice is yours
It always has been

Dancing With The Devil

Mother's intuition exists

I'll never forget the day I matured

The day my innocence was taken

Sex didn't take my innocence

Sex didn't mature me

Sex wasn't involved

I sat on his lap and I felt him aroused

It made me confused

He did nice things like put berets in my hair

It made me happy

I sat in his room alone and we cuddled on his couch

It made me comfortable

And then it happened

He looked in his pants and I was confused again

He talked about how it was getting bigger and I was intrigued

He locked the door

I was a child and he was a teenager

I asked him to see what he was looking at and I'll never forget when he did

My innocence crushed

He didn't have sex with me but it was gone

He didn't touch me but I felt violated

I told him mine didn't look like that and he asked me what it did look like

I undressed for him and showed him my body

My mother knocked on the door and tried to come in
She shouted and everything seemed blurry
I covered myself with a blanket not knowing what else to do
I thought I was in trouble
I was afraid to move
And I'll never not be afraid
My mother saved my life and I'll never forget it
That is how I know mother's intuition exists

The Day I Broke

You'll forget about me
As days pass
And clocks tick
Eventually
It will be as if
I never existed

Stopwatch

The shades are drawn and I shudder
My nightlight clicks but I'm still in darkness
It's always around me everywhere I go
The monster under my bed
His hands always on me
His eyes always watching
I never sleep
Morning comes and the sun creeps in
Always tired
He keeps me up every night
Even in my dreams he lurks
Waiting for the shades to be drawn
Everyone fast asleep
But not me
Not the monster
Floor boards creek
He comes again
His claws sink in and pull me under
Under the blankets
Into his world
I can't escape

Monster

I scrub the surface of my skin everyday

My only peace

Exfoliate

I never feel fully clean

Wipe tears from my face

I still feel them on my cheeks

Smiles make your face cramp

Unfamiliar feeling

Biting nails and cuticles

Anxiety and overeating consume me

Never go outside and forget what it's like to breathe

Fresh air hurts your face and the sun is blinding

Drink every night to keep the voices quiet

Mess

You lit the match
Watched in astonishment
As I burned away
The flames eat the flesh from my bones
Yet you're the one screaming for help
As you stand there unharmed
Free, skin intact
Yet I hear you scream
As if you're the one burning

"Victim"

It seems I've walked a million miles
My feet ache with every step
I haven't the slightest clue of where I'm headed
I can't remember where I'm from
Or even my own name
All I know is I keep walking
Till I find something to claim

Displaced

You are the anchor that pulls me to the bottom of the sea.
I am but a single wave trying to stay with your forever changing current
Alone in this vast water, not a soul to calm me
I go with the flow of unpredictable tides
Will someone throw me a lifeline?
Or shall I endure the endless deep with you?

Clownfish

I'm mad at myself

I let you rule my land

For so long

I forgot it was mine

I let your voice

Overtake mine

I forgot how many octaves I could sing

I let you change me

Into something I wasn't

Till I lost that person in the facade

I let your anger creep into my bones

I forgot how peaceful life could be

I gave you my love

My body

My soul

My home

And you just took

But I let you

And I'll never forgive myself

I Let You

Why do I do this

Make a mess

Never clean

Undress

Repeat

Repress

What I feel

Drink it all away

Forget to eat

As if I can change who I am

Deep inside

All lies

Covered in pretty tongues

Of whoever will get close to me

Whore

I want to not feel this way

So helpless over you

A pain I thought I'd escaped

When I pushed you from my view

All the words you used to say

Twist into me

Rusty screws

Ruled by the fear you fused into my veins

Though you never left a bruise

PTSD

Take them all away from me
All the tears
Every feeling
Take it all until there's nothing left
But numbness
And clean bones
Decomposed
One with the earth's soil

Fertilizer

I'll probably be crying myself to sleep
For the rest of my life
Maybe not always
Not every night
But I don't think it will ever fade
Forever scarred
So afraid of the pain
That I'll never be okay

Wet Pillows

And you said, over and over
As if it would change my mind
"No one will ever love you, the way I do"
I pray you're right
Because that's the last thing I want

Fake Love

It tends to swallow

The empty

Lonely void

The water is shallow

And still

I am drowning

Being washed down

No longer whole

So close

Grazing the edge of the end

With my fingertips

Every second

I breathe

And I feel

Like I'm gone already

I have been

For so long

Vacant

Gone

Keep pouring till my vision blurs
Till I sleep without a fight
Anything to make the thoughts slur
And quiet for the night

Merlot

Dealing with you
Because I have to
Like so many others
A curse, if you will
No matter how far I run
Into the arms
Of seemly full hearted people
They always leave me crumbling
Even the ones
Who swore to protect me
They gave me their hearts off their sleeve
And yet I couldn't see
Through fogged glass of your cage's walls
That it was a fake heart you forged
From pieces of trash that gusted in your winds
You covered it in paint and gold flakes
Wrapped it in a pretty bow
Dressed it up just enough
To fool me into believing
Once again
I'd found safety

One Man's Trash Is Another Fool's Treasure

You left me
After I handed you my heart
Like my love was free
As if what we had wasn't worth fighting for
You left me
When I needed you
Just to come back
And demand my love
Now, my dear
The price is too high
And you haven't got the coin

Abandoned

CHAPTER II

THE STORM

You carry the weight of the world
Resting on your shoulders
Carving grooves into your skin
So many things you want to say
And yet you hold it all in
Is it for the better?
To pretend and to leave it unsaid
It feels like forever
And as the end nears
It's a conversation you dread
Afraid of the outcome
Fearful of the unknown
In the end it's worth it
Embrace the pain and just let go

Open Your Mouth

I will push it away
The pain
The pit
In my chest
My heart
Even if it crushes me
I won't let it take me
I will make it through
The darkness
The emptiness
I will fill it with light
Until it's gone

Fighter

There are days that feel eternal
Days I want to scream
Pull my hair out of my scalp
Walk away and just breathe
Trying so hard not to lose it
Maintain some sanity
Pulling all the weight
Alone, so frustrating
When asking for help is weakness
And searching for love is exhausting
Find strength inside yourself
Instead of waiting for something
You can build your own happiness
After all, people are disappointing

Look Within

Hold on
To hoping it will get better
Even if there's nothing
If it seems impossible

Hold onto anything
Within your grasp
To keep you on solid ground
Even if it feels
As if its cracking beneath you

Sometimes things are more
More than they seem
Sometimes you're so far in the dark
You just forget what the light feels like

Hold on
It can get better
There's always something
It may be small
So small you forget it
The sound of your friends laughing

Your pet rubbing against your leg
The colour of the sky when it sets
It may be just a second
But it's something
Worth holding onto

Don't Let Go

Let go and proceed
You don't need to feel needed
Follow your own lead
Leave it behind and look forward

Better Things

Focusing on yourself

Is not egotistical

But a priority

Necessity

There's nothing wrong

With building your empire

From the ground

To the heavens

With your own

Two hands

Relishing your time

Enjoying your comforting seclusion

Zero distractions

Fixated on paramountcy

Self-reliance

A mere peasant is all I am to you
Yet you call me your queen
A queen should be on a pedestal
Not down in the dirt
A queen deserves a king
Strong and supportive
Continuously disappointed
You don't deserve a crown

I Deserve More

Open your eyes
See the world in front of you
Release the pain of the past
Move forward, look ahead
Never backwards
Forgive yourself for what you've done
You're allowed to make mistakes
Forget the person you once were
You'll never have to be them again
Accept the fate of what will be
You don't have control anyways
See the worth you hold in your hands
It's so much more than you believe

Worthy

You can, will it

Transcend

Have patience

You're strong enough

Relinquish the pain

And progress

Reincarnate

Be better

Say goodbye

Look forward

Let go of what was

Never regret

No one is perfect

Take the steps

Make the climb

Never stop, no time

Reach the top

You can

Final

There's this block
Inside my head
It tries to stop me
It tells me I'm lost
That I'm missing pieces
I'm not enough
Not strong

But I say
You're wrong
I'm exactly where I need to be
In as many pieces
As necessary
Just strong enough
Who I am
Found

Enough To Break You

My walls stay up
Forever guarding
What's left of me
Tired of restarting
Lock all the doors
Throw away the keys
Because in the end
Everyone leaves

Safe Than Sorry

Why can't you see
The pain you inflict
The words you say
How they tear me apart
Why can't you hear
My silent cries for help
Or even the loudest ones
Why cant you be who you were
Who I fell so deep for
Who now I fear
Is just a figment of my imagination
And when you do finally see
It'll be too late

Facade

I can't bring myself
To open up
Open my heart
Give away my precious time
Get close
Comfortable
Fall profoundly
Immerse myself in a life
With someone by my side
Let alone settle, marry
I can't
The risk is too high
To relive the worst moment
Where I lost so much
To do it again would be fatal
Especially with someone
I've given everything to
Just for them to take it

When They Go

I would bear all the pain in the world
Break my spine
Carry it on my shoulders
Let my bones snap as I collapse
If it would make you happy
Even just for a moment

Sacrifice

You can call me wrong

The villain

Like I'm the one who broke us

And point all the fingers

Pin everyone against me

That will take your words over mine

You've already talked over me the whole time

Getting my point across is pointless

You can't reason with stubborn and stupid

Bad Guy

I know I have to let you go
The healthy choice
Imperative to my survival
We're too different
I should have seen
How I give all I am
And you watch me
Staying whole
Remaining untouched
Doing what you want
While I sacrifice my love

Stagnant

I'm where I belong
Even if I'm breaking
Crying
Hurting
Being crushed
By my own thoughts
The words I hear

His eyes that look down on me
Into the dirt
Beneath the earth
I'm where I'm supposed to be
Even if I feel trapped
Alone
Afraid to move

One day
I'll be where I'm meant to stay
I know that, deep down
In the aching bones I walk with
In my heart that palpates
In response to loud noises

I'll get there
If it takes months
Years, even
I'll find my happy place
My forever home

Everything happens for a reason

It will hurt more than anything
Letting you go
Watching you love another
Giving them what I should have had
What I thought I deserved
It will hurt more than anything
To give the love I gave you
To someone else
But one day the pain will cease
One day we'll both be happy
Where we're meant to be
Apart

Hurt

It's hard living in a world
Where you want love so desperately
But you can't accept it
Even when it's right in front of you
You push it away
Because you've lost before
Fear overcomes optimism
So you remain, solely desolate

Philophobia

Try to feel happy

When the sun shines down

Soak in the rays

Serotonin

Smile all day

Even start to believe

For a second

That I'm okay

Make Believe

I tried so hard
With all my being
Not to scar
Or hurt anyone's feelings
But it's not about me
Or you, even
But about the person
Who gave our lives meaning
I never wanted to tear
What we had to pieces
I even lived a lie
For years
Forever dreaming
Wishing I was elsewhere
That I was someone I'm not
That I could be myself
Or the fear would be gone
Your shadow was heavy
Weighing me down
Even the biggest smiles
Couldn't hide my frown
I wasn't the best
I could be
Not for you
Or him

Or even me
I wanted to be more
Be someone he can look up to
He could only look down at me
If I stayed next to you
I hope one day we can look back
And that you'll understand
I would have given anything
To still love the man
Who gave me the greatest gift
Despite the days that grew sad
The pain is irrelevant
We can be good without the bad

Battle

I want to break through
That glass ceiling
That weighs me down
Telling me I'm not enough
That I can't make it on my own
Without a man by my side
Pulling my strings
Writing my verses for me
As if I don't have a voice
Or my own muscles to move
Just a pawn in their game
Forever wanting to choose

Hidden

I should never have gotten so used
To the sounds of your screams
To the flailing of your arms
Or the way you talked down to me
Your arrogance shouldn't be
Customary
In fact, it should be obsolete
Yet you wondered why I gave up on
What we could have been
We were transforming and couldn't see
The bitterness in every sin
The resentment that built each day
How you transferred this anger unto me
A taste of your own medicine
I thought it may help, but it only
Broke me

Becoming The Monster

I'm ready for the change
To pull the trigger
Execute
Move on to something else
Maybe bigger, better
Even lesser
As long as I never settle
For something under my worth

Photosynthesis

Waiting for the world to move again
For it to spin and force me around
For time to pass and to forget
The days that have no end
The dread that lingers in my mind
Waiting to move
To step out of the dark
For the scenery to change
And this aching to leave my heart
I'm waiting for the world to move again
For myself to grow
Out of the shell I can't fit anymore
For my mind to just know
This is where I change
Where I evolve

Cultivate

I've always chased this feeling
What I thought was love
But I think was mainly just acceptance
I've been on dating apps
Went on bad dates
Some good ones
Had one night stands
Friends with benefits
Fell in love
Broke hearts
Nothing ever felt concrete
Only one
And that was terrifying
So I fell back
In fear that I'd ruin the friendship I had
With someone so special
Even still
Nothing felt natural
Or unforced
Or painless
It all just felt like it was missing something
So I don't chase that feeling anymore
I'm not chasing someone who may or may not exist
Because let's face it
Being alone is just as difficult as being with someone

And being with someone who isn't right for you
Well
It may be a learning experience
It may bring you joy for a while
But it always ends up exhausting
And I'm tired of losing
Tired of breaking
Tired of looking
Even waiting
I'll just be here
Letting nature run its course

Natural, Love

It may take me years
To find the voice I lost
But when I do
I shall shout from the highest of rooftops
And not a single soul
Could silence me

Projecting

You gave me inches
I gave you yards
Maybe that wasn't fair
To request the ocean
From someone who could only spare droplets
Of dirty rain water
When I'd go out of my way
To purify my tears for you
Perhaps I was being selfish
Expecting my water to be clean
Assuming what you offered
In the beginning
Still stood tall like trees

You Can't Find You In Someone Else

I just can't win
With this brain of mine
Resembling a brick wall
Covered with vines
Always trying to grow
But never getting through
Going every which way
Eventually, you enjoy the view
Accept the fact that these walls remain
That, even though you are changing
You still stay the same
Flowers will blossom
Till you're covered, anew
Maybe the walls aren't so bad
Just enjoy being you

Let Yourself Grow

Even after the many days
And night hours
I've spent suffering
Crying
Begging not to feel
Anything
Even after I've screamed
Into pillows
The same ones
That my caught my tears
Even after I shutter at the sounds
Of passing cars
Loud music
Sudden screams of strangers
Even after I catch myself
Still letting you have power
Over me
Like I fought tooth and nail to get out
For nothing
And still am fighting
I probably will be
Until I die
Yes, even after all these things
You put me through
I suppose I owe you thanks

You taught me what not to take
You taught me how to put my foot down
You taught me how to plug my ears
You taught me what love is not
But most importantly you gave me a gift
A gift to turn every minuscule piece
Of this tragedy, Into art

Student

It's okay to look back

Every now and then

As long as you stay forward

No straying from the path ahead

Reminiscing

There is not a soul
Too good
For the likes of you
You are a treasure
Pure gold
Unlike all others
Authentic and true

Gold

Stop explaining yourself

You don't owe anyone an explanation

For anything, ever

You're allowed to take your time

To cancel plans

Ignore calls

Cut someone out

If their addition to your life isn't healthy

The only person you owe anything to is you

Put Your Foot Down

Healing takes time

You wish you could rush it

Fast forward

Go past all the hard times

Skip the journey

Reach the destination

With nothing to show

No scars or stories to tell

No dirt under your fingernails

But, you need to get your hands dirty

Earn your keep

Fight through the barrier

That holds you in place

That stops you from feeling

You need to feel the pain

In order to learn to bear it

And once you do that

You can bear anything

Embrace your scars

Befriend the hurt

Enjoy every second

Till you learn, what it's worth

Pain Is Necessary

Never again will your name
Be heard from my voice
I hope you sit around loathing
Wishing you made the right choice
I won't wait around to be chosen
When you're lonely at night

I'm Not A Fucking Bat

You'll miss my touch
And the taste of my lips
The way I traced your skin
With my fingertips
You'll miss my laugh
And the sound of my voice
The last time I said "goodnight"
Will haunt your every choice

Friday Nights

I feel like I have no one
Because the people
Who are right next to me
Feel so fucking far away
They just use me
To make them look good
Like I'm some charity
Act like they love me
While they hold hands
With my enemies
You're supposed to be my support
But you're the anchor
Waiting on my lungs to seize

In The Weeds

I must destroy her
I know, I must
But I fear with her
The rest of me will follow
She sits in my heart
And toys with my strings
I have to cut her out
Like rotting tissue
Spreading disease
If I want to grow
To be better
She has to go
And never look back

Break The Cycle

I dig, endlessly

For something shiny

Something new

Something old

Dirt flies over my shoulders

With it, it feels like I've lose more pieces

On the way to find them, as if I'm running in place

Without destination

Always digging

Finding nothing

Just the same broken glass that used to hold me in place

The same skeletons I thought I buried deeper

Dig, dig, dig

Hoping to find my old self

The corpse I left behind

All those years ago

Her flesh has become one with the earth

Yet, I feel her heartbeat in the cold ground

So I dig, endlessly

Forgetting that I'm standing here

Without her

All on my own

Gravedigger

I let you get under my skin
I let you destroy me
Bury into my arteries
Control my mind
Alter my thoughts
Manipulate my feelings

You are the definition of abuse
Yet you are so irresistible
Put me down a million feet
In the ground I lay
Trying to dig to the surface
Suffocating in my own mind

Attempt to escape
But I am here again
In the soil, entwined in your roots
Constructed by your insults
Yet flowers still bloom from my grave
Somehow even in the coldest of weather
A lone flower blooms
Out of a crack in the concrete
The concrete you've laid down on top of me

So much weight I can barely hold it
And even though my muscles tense
As my shoulders shake
I can almost feel my bones crack
The weight is held
Another day
Another week
Months and years go by
Beneath the concrete I lay
For an eternity it seems

Some days you are like fertilizer
Helping me grow tall
Other days you forget to water me
Leaving me wilted and weak
Your mood swings twist my insides
Like a corkscrew in my gut

I am trapped
I am not safe with you
Yet I feel at home in your arms
I want to be free of your hold
Even still, I don't want you to let go
The confusion keeps me captive
In your dying garden

But through the roots I feel a pulse
Something new brewing

The crack in the concrete grows
As do the flowers
My self worth that was once diminished
Rebuilds like a fortress
And though I love the way your roots wrap around me
I tear them off and start to dig
Up and out of this grave you've buried me in
Out of the concrete that is you

My finger nails break and bleed as I claw my way out
Bleeding is worth it to be free, however
Covered in blood I am
But that is how I was meant to be
For I am a red daisy
One which you once held so tight
To the point of asphyxiation

But you, like all holders of red daisies
Are oblivious to the power we hold
And that is the downfall of the concrete
Ignorance to the thing you say you love

A red daisy can only crave the concrete for so long
Until one day they break through
And grow into their own garden
A terrace without cement
An oasis that flourishes

Concrete may be strong
But in time it crumbles
Cold and hard
Used to being walked on
Is that why you buried me?
So you wouldn't be alone in the dark?

That is no excuse to crush me
Palms drenched in my blood
I let you in my veins
In hopes you'd give me strength
You are the one that is weak
The one who belongs in the dirt
Release my soul so I can bloom

Red Daisy

CHAPTER III

THE FOREST

Where did the time go?
Everything flew by
A gust of wind
Dandelions blow
Away like my memories
Fading more every second
Faint reminders
Trigger happy moments
It's almost as if I'm disappearing
Translucent

Forgetting

I don't think I'll ever be normal

Be able to stop feeling

All the pain for others

For myself

Pain for those who don't even exist

I'll never be able to live

In just one world

My mind just doesn't work that way

I crave more

Adventure

Purpose

Thrill

Things I can't find in my small world

All the things I want and will never have

So I'll close my eyes and escape

To a new world

Full of possibilities

Happiness

Sadness

Even more pain

Then write it all down

And make my dreams come true

Writing Forever

Why should it matter?
The colour of my eyes
Or the skin I wear
Or the gender I feel like fucking
The music that makes me want to dance
Does it make me that different from you?
That it makes your skin crawl at night
Tell me
How does it possibly affect your life
You think it's hate
Hatred in your veins
But you can't handle anything outside your white picket fence
It is fear that drives you
Fear that drives the hate you spew out of your mouth
Can you not handle something new?
A new taste on your tongue
Something exciting that opens your eyes
Of course not
Stay in your small fenced in world
We don't have room for weakness in ours anyways

Close-minded

Lost in it
In the facade
Living a lie
Too far gone
This love is a myth
A master of pretending
My profession
So condescending

Two Faced

I'll wish you best
Even though you fucking sucked
Cause even the worst people
Deserve to be loved

Bittersweet

No one talks about the darkest days
We just stay silent
Pretend it doesn't exist
Wear the mask, hide away
Tuck ourselves in
Sleep it off
Repeat

Live in the falsities
We create
Our own little worlds
Where we get to be someone
More appealing
Receive some attention
We crave but won't allow
In the real world

It never makes you feel better
Only prolonging the inevitable
We do it again and again
Hiding behind the persona
In hopes no one sees what's underneath

Interweb

It's terrifying
Looking in the mirror
And not recognizing who you see
Your body feeling like a foreign land
Eyes forever meet the floor
Because you're ashamed of your skin
Wishing you could shed it like a snake
And be something new

Slither

I don't want to be like you
Delusional, dishonest
Do you actually believe the lies you tell?
You are an imposter
Try to play the victim
But you are the one swinging the blade
And yet no one sees
Only I can see through your mask
See the filth underneath
Fake your way through life
Like you always have
I try not to be like you
Be honest, true
Holding back the urge to be human
But it's in my blood
Flows through my veins
Your words become my own
We share the same name
I'll keep fighting it
Until the day I die
I won't be like you
All I can do is try

Mask

Red hot skin, scorching face
Far away from home, my feet in the dirt
This open field with so much space
But nowhere to run
A flock of crows above my head
My eyes burn from the sun
Sweat dripping down my brow
Clothes sticking to my skin
Waiting in this heat for hours
Would you please just let me in
I'm melting into my bones
Never stop moving
Shovels over shoulders
Pounds, forever losing
Can never shake your hunger
Or the aching in your feet
You hold in so much anger
Yet are forced to endure defeat

Enslaved

Wash away your sins
With the blood you've spilled
You'll never be forgiven
Every thought lingers
With a blade to your throat
You belong in the dark
Alone at last
You'll always belong to the cold dead
Known it since you opened your eyes
There's nothing for you here
It clouds your mind
That sadness creeps in
And with it, shadows
Shadows that whisper
In your ear
In your heart
Breaking down every muscle
And corrupting your instincts
No longer trusting your gut
Would you let them slit your throat
So you could feel, just once?

Flesh

You could give me
All the love in the world
And it still couldn't fill
The hole he left
I'll still miss his voice
And the way he smiled
How he taught me
How to love
I will always feel empty
Searching for anything
To satiate that wound
Even if you are the light
And shines me to a path
I'd still find myself
Craving the night

Grieving

Thankful

They say that's what you should be

As if it's something you can just program

Into you brain

As if you can just lay a cover

On the overwhelming weight

Watch it disappear

Like magic

You have everything

You should feel grateful, right?

Nothing should be heavy to you

As if a spotlight

Can make you less human

Spotlight

To the boy next door who wanted to play house
Did it make you feel like a "daddy"?
To the men who yell from the bar patio
Did it make your day to see me shiver?
To the men who holler from passing cars
Do you enjoy my middle finger?
That family friend that scarred me forever
Did you like seeing me naked?
To the girls that forced me to kiss a boy
Did you enjoy ruining a first for me, just because you could take it?

It made you feel strong, powerful
It made me weak, fearful
Of men and little girls alike
It made me disgusted to be a human
It made me hate my body
I put up walls for years
It left me confused
I lost myself trying to find who I was
And I'll keep trying to overcome those feelings for the rest of my life
I can't change the way it made me feel
Not ever
But I can chose to be better

Better than the ones who broke me
Stronger than they'll ever be

Overcome

A million words could leave my lips
In a hundred different octaves
Every tone my voice could make
Would never reach your eardrums
You'd prefer to hear any other voice
To turn a blind eye to the world around you
You sat on the shore with your feet up
While I sank into the ocean

SOS

I know it won't hurt so much
Eventually
I'll never forget
But it will become easier
Right?
I can breathe in
And out
Without panicking
Remembering you won't hurt
It will be a comfort
Right?
I can look back
On days you were here
Without my eyes tearing up
Look at these pictures
Without wanting to rip them up

Bereaved

Heart beating

Blood thickens

Palpitations

Sweat dripping

Run away

Feet aching

Eyes water

Breathtaking

Gasping for air

Trembling shakes

Screaming and shout

Bones break

Lost for words

Only "help"

No one can hear you

No way out

Fear

Hiding in plain sight
A master of disguise
I cover it up with makeup
You think everything is fine
I'm ripe like a peach
Ready for picking
Pick me up off the floor
But you never stop kicking
You say that you'll change
But you only hit harder
Run rabbit, run away
Your love, too precious to barter
But my heart made of wax
It melts for your fire
Dripping on the floor like tears
The tears you cry, perfect liar
Will I ever be free?
From this unending hold
Will the scars ever heal
Or your heart turn from cold?
Lies that sound like the truth
Your serpent tongue keeps me guessing
I know I'm bound for damnation with you
Yet I stop myself from progressing
In a casket I lay awaiting my sentence

Over top of me you stand
Your shadow making me breathless
Just as the tight grip of your hands

Beaten

Separate my flesh from my aching bones
Peel back the layers one by one
Gather the blood that spews
Remove each broken fingernail
And pull out each tooth
Clean my skin and make me good as new
Sew my teeth together so I never speak again
Fit me in my favourite red dress
Put me on display for my family to see
Their tears fall on my cold, powdered cheeks
Though no one can see me
Screaming inside a rotting shell
"I'm still here"
But no one hears me
I am stiff and numb, but I am still here
Lost inside myself, not alive or dead
It is as dark as one may fear
Dad kisses my forehead

In Between

Stupid

Is all I am

Regret

Is all I feel

Belonging

Is all I want

What is it, to feel like you've made the right choice?

How do you come to peace with that choice once it's made?

Where do you find a home in a wasteland?

Open arms

Do they exist?

For someone like you

Someone who second guesses every step

And rejects any sense of normalcy

Happiness

Is it real?

Will you ever taste the tongue of someone who isn't your specially made poison?

Tears

Will they ever stop?

Is there anyone out there to wipe them away?

Love

Will you ever truly know what it means?

Is there a human being on this earth that shows you what it really is?

That's the problem, isn't it

Reliance

If you can't find it in you, you'll never find it anywhere else

Mirror

Is there a planet somewhere out there
That better suits me
That will make me feel like I'm not
An extraterrestrial
Gravity crushing me
Like waves of lead
I don't belong here

Take Me To Your Leader

Call me unholy
Because I don't bow to your god
The same god
Who allows evil people
To praise his name
I'd rather remain godless
Than follow as another wolf
In sheep's clothing

Unholy

I'll never forget the moment
You stopped breathing
How your eyes already looked
As if you were sleeping
You were so sedated
So far gone
But it felt like you were there
Like you waited for us
I'll never forget how it felt
All the tears
My lack of words
I wanted to say so much
All I could mutter
Was "i love you"
And I never got closure
I never got grieve
Life was just to busy
I've always been better at burying things
But I'll still think of you
Every time January hits
And as the rain freezes over
Another year
I'll be wishing I did

Roy

I've waited a lifetime

To see you crumble

In your shadow I waited

To see you regret every time you've hurt me

I wanted to feel stronger

To feed off your pain

But when I saw it first hand

There was nothing to gain

Just a broken man laying in his own self pity

I wanted to laugh but only felt shame

How is it that I can feel for this monster?

As if I'm just made of stupidity

To you this was only a game

You tore me apart

Left nothing to be claimed

I was your puppet, moving every which way

You played the pawn

Pointing fingers after you drove me insane

And yet here I am, sharing the blame

I was also the monster

I didn't see it in time

I'm sorry for what I've done, but can you say the same?

Yin And Yang

I did everything he wanted
And every time I did
It took a piece of me
A piece I'll never get back
Over and over
I gave myself away
Till only a sliver remained
Nothing but an insignificant fragment
The closest thing to nothing
Is still something
Isn't it?

I'm Something, I guess

This can't be it
I refuse to believe it
It's not the end for me
I won't die without meaning
I can't let go of this world
When so much is left unfinished
Who will lay down my words
When the worms eat my flesh?

A Writer's Last Words

Drinking wine
Straight from the bottle
Hoping I'll drown
In its spirit before my own tears
I tell everyone I'm alright
But I would give anything
For you to be here

Getting Through It

I wear black year round
It makes me feel warm
Coloured hair
Chains on my neck
I love the looks
From the Karen's of the world
They look down on me
As if they're high and mighty
Because they wear a cross
Nevertheless
I smile their way
Kill them with kindness
As my mother would say

Wild One

I play your favourite song
On repeat
Makes me feel like
You're still with me
Is it pathetic?
Maybe
I still haven't washed my sheets
Just wanna lay here
Until the sun sleeps
Can't remember
The last time I wanted to eat
I'll just keep listening
Close my eyes and feel your body heat
Hear your voice
Soft and sweet

Something's Missing

The night is where I feel alive

In its bleakness

Hypnotized

Where I can dance

Be myself

Stripped to the bone

Basked in moonlight

Night Owl

In deep forest I grow in isolation
With entwining roots embedded in the dirt
Fungi surround me, a carcass of meat
Moss, my clothing I wear proud
The birds sing songs for me
As they peck out my eyes
Worms entangled in my hair
I am a sacrifice to mother nature
A beautiful corpse on display in her wood
Becoming one with the earth I walked on
With bare feet I felt its energy
Surrender to her and let her take me
Beetles make a home in my belly
And spiders lay eggs in my mouth
Cherish me as you would your creatures
The same ones that feed off my flesh
Howl at the moon just for me
Let the moonlight glow upon me
The circle of life

Goblin

You deserve love
To be adored
Everything you want
Should be yours
You may have to fight
Travel around the globe
Until you find it
If you do
Keep it close
Even if it feels foreign
Or like water that's too hot
Accept it
Let yourself adjust
But never forget
The steps you took
Tears you wept
The long nights you shook
You gave so much of yourself
for this moment
Don't let it pass
Because of trivial fear
Never forget you earned it

Deserve

Feel like a burden
When you ask for help
Tell yourself
It's just the cards you were dealt
It's your weight to carry
Just as the pain you've felt
With every day that buries
You farther into yourself

Motherly

Sitting here like an idiot

Crying over you

Even though I never got a chance

To hold you

Or feel your flesh

All it took was your words

To steal my heart

And make me whole

You were miles away

But I always felt you

Right here

And now we're worlds apart

Maybe in another life

I can repay the favor

1:32AM

Does it really matter?

The time we waste

Or food we eat

Who we decided to kiss

The words we speak

As long as they're sweet

Who are we to judge one another?

Were we all made from a similar mold?

I think not

I think we are all perfectly different

And we can lead our different lives in different ways

And everyone should just mind their own fucking business

Turn a blind eye like they do with dead natives

Or anti-maskers and save our children

Pretend that people who aren't the same color as you

Do not exist

While you judge women for flaunting their tits

As if you don't enjoy seeing our bodies

Build your empires on stolen lands

Pile up coffins

All in the name of our Lord and Savior

Put money in a basket to fuel all the hatred

Blind

Talking about what took you
Sickens me
It's all around
In the air we breathe
Constant reminders
Of masks on passing faces
Deep seeding regret
And rising cases
If I could have taken it from you
And gave it to myself
Someone strong enough
With better health
I would have done anything, really
Anything to save you
But, I was weak
Full of rage
Selfish as I am
I didn't want to
Face that you were giving in
This was your last page
You didn't want to live
And I needed you to
Here I go, being selfish again

What You Wanted

I wish that I could kick it
This codependent liquid
That makes the world shine brighter
When everything seems so dim

Liquid Courage

It's like a switch in your brain
We all have it
Even those who are pure inside
There's always something
That just tips you over the edge
And then you lose control
Of who you are
And what's right
It's just missing for a moment
But by the time you realized that
It's too late
You've gone too far
And there's no going back

When You Snap

Do you ever just feel like the world is made of plastic? Sugar coated in sprinkles and frosting made of artificial ingredients, nothing is real here. Not even time. Not even me. Not even my heart and the way it trembles while I stare at my ceiling wishing I could fit into a plastic mold like everyone else. I feel like I'm made of wood and leaves and dirt like I grew from what we were originally and everyone around me is just another store bought plant made of styrofoam and felt. They look so pretty on the outside and they'll last forever as I wither away and dry up but at least I smelled like the earth and served a short purpose, a pure purpose that made someone smile just for a minute, at least I was real.

Dead Flower

After a long dark night
Beyond the fog that lingers
Down a fallen leaf path
Crisp and crunchy
Through the misty woods
The moon lays down
All the shadows disappear
Over a hill draped in dark
A small light peaks
Basking all in its path
In warmth that is yellow
Flowers open to say hello
Whispers silence and sound grows
A layer of dew covers all green
Waking up all unseen

Sunlight

Mother nature has given us a gift
The earth her canvas
So much beauty to be seen
From ash and mud spread across it
Carved into wood
Hand prints in the sand
Crackle of the fire
Smoke filling the sky
The wind howls in the night
Moonlight shone on lush meadows
Birds sing in the morning
Trees sway and creak
Leaves fall and shower the earth
Waves crash against ample stones
Rain pours as flowers grow
It's all connected
Sewn together through soil
This gift we've been given
And we only destroy it

Planet Earth

Falling from the sky
The air still
Chills up my spine
Slicing my skin
Landing on ice
I expected your arms
Catching me below
You're nowhere to be seen
I'll sink into the snow
Freeze over
Fossilized
Embrace the cold
Trust is my demise

Trust Fall

CHAPTER IV

THE SUNLIGHT

I'll fall into place
In that I have faith
I could close my eyes
Knowing full well
I'll land into the right arms
No more second guessing
Be exactly where I am supposed to be
Embrace amenity
Knowing you're there to catch me

Landing

Nothing compares to you
My love, My best friend
You are everything I've been searching for
Making me whole when I feel broken
And making me strong when I feel weak
I never knew how much I needed you
Not until my heart broke
You picked up all the pieces
And your smile glued them back together
I brought you into this world
Because I needed you to lead me out of the dark
To hold my hand through all the bad
And you did
You saved me from myself
I promise you, for the rest of my days
I will never let go
I'll be there when you need me
To pull you out of the dark
To fight the bad
Nothing compares to you, my love

Knight In Shining Armor

Trying to find the best
Within the worst
The light inside the dark
The sun behind the moon
The remedy within the pain
Trying to find the best
Within myself, my worst self
Who I'm trying not to be
Fighting the urge to break
Searching for the glue to mend the pieces
I know it's all here
Locked away
Somewhere I forgot
Deep in the vast black
The black that shrouds my heart
It's there, I know it is
My light
My best
And I'm not going to stop searching
Until I find her

Never Lose Your Light

I'll love you until the end of my days
Your lies
Your secrets
Your pain
Your beauty
Your vanity
The way you make me insane
I'll love you until the end of my days
No matter what
That's the promise I made
Not because I'm lost without you
Not because I need you
Because I can't see my life without you
Even if it means bearing the pain
Until the end I'll love you

Committed

Craving your skin
Between my teeth
The touch of your lips
The way you breathe
My guilty pleasure
You always make me feel better

Stay Forever

Once in a lifetime, love
Something you'll never find again
Over generations it changes
But always remains timeless

Vintage, if you will

Learn to love yourself
When you make mistakes
When you say the wrong thing
When you don't do enough
Learn you cherish your body
Every scar
Every hair
Every stretch mark
Every curve
Accept you for who you are
All the tears
The anger
The jealousy
You are human
Forgive yourself
For every lie you spoke
Every promise you broke
All the hearts you hurt
You are more than your mistakes
You are better today than yesterday
You can grow
You can always be more
Learn to love yourself

Acceptance

You were born from ashes
Ashes that once were fire
That burned in the core of my heart
That could have destroyed everything
You were born from a piece of hope
Clinging to the idea that change was possible
And even though it was not
We still got you
The greatest gift of all
But it will never be your fault
That the stars didn't align for us
It is not your burden to bear
You were born from ashes
Not ones that blow away in the wind
Ones that will mould together
You will build, not destroy
You will conquer
And I will stand at your side
Through every decision
Because that fire I once held is now yours
And you will wield It in my name
You will be stronger than I ever could be
And I will always be proud of you

The Boy Made Of Flames

Our memories will forever remain
Tiny pieces of something once whole
They may be apart
But they're where they need to be

Growing Apart

One day

I tell myself

Over and over

Until I believe it

One day

I'll feel what they feel

With someone who deserves me

Deserves my love

My effort

My touch

One day

I'll find you

And I'll keep you close

And never let you go

Who Deserves Me

Sweet as candy
Tender lips
Tranquil touch
Of fingertips
Through my hair
Soft as silk
Drink you down
Thick as milk

Sweetheart

I know you're out there
Living your life
I wonder if you think of me
If you lay awake at night
Dreaming of me
Someone you don't know

We haven't yet met
But somehow it grows
This surety inside
That you're out there waiting
The perfect hand that fits mine
The perfect lips I've been craving

Arms that hold me tight
Eyes that make me weak
Words I hang onto
Every time you speak
A voice that makes me tremble
Like the sweetest song I've ever heard

Something I could listen to forever
Even screaming, even slurred
A love I would never question
Where I am safe to be myself

Something that feels destined
The surest thing I've ever felt

Soulmate

Pools of honey
Warm and runny
A hot summer day
Bright and sunny
Takes my breath away
Makes me hotter than the sun
Every time I look into your eyes
I know you're the one

Brown Eyes

There is a special place
For you to reside
In the cavity of my chest
The deepest, darkest nooks
Places I thought would never see light
Somewhere forgotten
That no one else deserves
Only you
You can stay there
As long as you like
The door is locked
And only you hold the key

It's Warmer Inside

I took you for granted
The way you loved
Gentle touch
Eyes in awe
When they looked at me
Every second like magic
I never knew
How hard it would be
To find your love
Without you

Irreplaceable

I held you there, inside my womb

Keeping you safe and warm

Feeding you and waiting

It wasn't until I held you in my arms

That I knew true love existed

I looked into your eyes and I knew

You were the only one to capture my soul

To hold my heart in your hands

Keep it forever my love

You're the only person on this earth that deserves it

I'll hold yours as long as I can

One day I know I'll have to let go

But you'll never have to return mine

It's forever yours

True Love

What am I supposed to do
With all this pounding in my chest
With how much I love being near you
Maybe accepting that, is my first test
And the second could be mastering
How to steady my breathing
In your presence I can't help it
Constantly overheating
I could write a list
Of the things I love about you
Like the gentle pressing of your lips
Or simple things that you do
How you slick your hair back with both hands
The way you tilt your head back when you laugh
All these little moments resonate with me
I just pray that it lasts

Here's To Hoping

I want to believe
That you are real
That the things I want
And what I feel
Is something possible
To concede
As if I stole
You from a dream

Daydream

I am trying to trust
The words you say aren't lies
To put all the past
And it's pain, aside
Remind myself
Not everyone is alike
None of the rest
Carry a softness
Like the one in your eyes
Even so
Within your gentle hands
I can't help but feel rigid
Despite the fact my broken pieces
Next to yours, feels splendid
Pain grows
Like it always has
Behind my ribs and in my chest
Fear always creeping in
Even though I feel my best
What if?
I end up alone
In this darkness again

Trying

So many words go through my head
When I see your face
I'm speechless
Uncontrollably
Unsaid
Every time you ask me
"What?"
All I can say, is
"You"

You

You're exactly what I've been missing
Choking and spanking
Always ends with us kissing
I always felt like I needed something
More than what I had
Which left me starving
And with you I never have to beg
Never finishes, always restarting
The match that lights my fire
Forever your darling

Heat

Will you bend or break me
Will you stick around
Will I forget your smell
Or your laugh
How I love that sound
Are you the one
The one to tie me down
Or will you turn and run
My heart into the ground

Bend Or Break

I love the way you look at me
Like I'm worth more than I feel
And I wish that you could see
The way my heart beats for you, surreal

Heartbeat

I built this home for you
With blood and sweat on my brow
Forged the walls from my very bones
Rolled up my sleeves
Got my hands dirty
My fingernails will be stained for eternity
And it is worth it

Anything that is within my grasp I will get for you
And anything beyond that, we will build a ladder to reach
Everything you want will be yours
I will see to it
If I have to break my back for you
I will do it
I would carry the moon on my shoulders
Just to see you smile

X

I'll write you little letters
Even though you'll never read them
I'll imagine what you'd say
As if you never left us
I'll talk to you as if you'll answer
And buy things you'll never try
Every time I think of you
I struggle not to cry
And even though my heart is broken
And my brain just won't work
I'll keep writing those letters
As if they're my last words

Dear Mama,

There is no form of measurement
To count the amount of love
My heart holds for you
You are the sun that brightens my day

Son

I promised myself
I'd wait to fall again
To work alone
Not get swept up in
Whatever it is
Your eyes seem to hold
From a single glance
I knew
That my heart could be sold
All you need is to ask
Everything could be yours
From the space between my fingers
To the key to my door

Unexpected

You're just passing time
And I'm still here
Hanging on a line
That will never draw you near
I ignored all the signs
Even though they were clear
All the interest was mine

My Dear

I wish you could see it
Sometimes
And then I don't
The world you left behind
All the beauty in it
Despite the pain
The stupidity
The Evil
Past all that
There's moments where
I think if you were here
You'd appreciate it
The songs you've never heard
The colors of the sunset from my side of the ocean
The moonlight on a foggy night
Flowers that bloom, the same day you left us
I wish you could see it
Just for a second

Missing You

I'm a mess
And you're so collected
Can't help but feel
I don't deserve
The love I'm being subjected

Too Good For Me

The sun

The moon

The stars

Have nothing on you

You shine brighter than them all

Sweet Summer Child

I fell in love with you
All of you
Every word that fell from your lips
Every silence we sat through
That wasn't awkward
Not even for one second
I fell in love with you
Before I even had the pleasure
Of touching your flesh
Or tasting your tongue
I fell in love with your soul
Even after you swore
Up and down that I couldn't
It was so beautiful
I couldn't bear to hate any bit of you
I fell so deeply
For all the things you hate
The things you swore may suffocate me
I would wait a lifetime
If I had to
To wait for you to see what I see

Perfection

Skin so soft

Warm to the touch

Lips that undo me

Fueled by your lust

Dark eyes that glue me

To my mattress

A slave to you

Anything you want

Firm hand around my throat

Please don't stop

One of a kind pleasure

Something you'd dream of

Where Have You Been All My Life?

Nothing will ever compare
To what it's like being with you
My love for you, complete
From the sun to the moon

The Sun To My Moon

It is in the depths
Of my loneliness
That I find serenity
Feels so familiar
Just like
When you were next to me
The only difference is
Loneliness never disappoints me
It's always the same
Strangely comforting

Singular

Feels like worlds apart
Even though it's just hours
Forever missing a piece
Whenever you're away
Wishing my fingers
Were entwined with yours
If only we didn't have to part
If only you could stay
No matter how far you go
It lingers
I'll love you until my last day

Distance

How do I tell you

That I want more

Without feeling

Like I'm ripping you away

How does one express

Something

Without ruining what already is

How can I show you

That this feeling is real

Behind all my fears

That I'd give you my heart

From my cold, dead chest

You have but to ask

And yet

Though every moment with you

Would be serene

Soft

Gentle

Happy

How can i possibly

Hand you the burden

That is me

How can I expect you

The one who deserves the red roses

You

The one who has given me the gift of motivation
You
The one who has always been
And always will
Keep this cold, dead heart beating
How can I expect you, to risk everything for me
Because I am a stick of dynamite
And you're the perfect match

Her

More than anything

I wish

I could give you my love

But I don't deserve yours

Even if I did

Losing you would be all too much

For me to bear

So I sit here

Daydreaming of what could be

What we could be

In our own world

Perfect

But that's the thing

Everything is perfect in your head

And on paper

Because in reality

I could break you

And that would break me

Just the thought does just that

How can I put you in that position

A position to be lost

I simply cannot

Lose You

I wish we could have grown together
Instead of bonding as adults
Not that I'd prefer you then
Rather know you better,, I suppose
It's sad that death brought us together
As many times as our faults
Maybe it's a cycle meant
To go on forever
Let's hope our children will be close

Brother

Hold me close
As I'm breaking
Pull together the pieces
My savior
Tell me you love me
Even though I'm a mess
Perhaps there's a God
Or whatever brought you to me
So lucky

So Blessed

Sweet sugar baby
I want you all to myself
But I'm stuck watching
While you love someone else
Maybe it's unfair of me
To expect anything in return
You've got the whole world
And I'd only make it burn
Just a silly little girl
With a silly little crush
You're still everything to me
Even if you'll never love me that much

Love him, love me not

You've got the perfect bit of sweetness
It balances with your feist
Much like the honey in your eyes
Can melt my heart made of ice
I never saw you coming
Even in the brightest light
You call me your angel
But I'm the devil in disguise
I'll never understand what you see in me
I'm just honored to call you mine

The Shadow and the Star

We were raised in the same Hell
Somehow managed to escape
I tried to fill the void
That stayed with you that day
I tried to forget your voice
And the smile on your face
The way your hair shined
In the summer sun
The perfect chestnut
I tried to erase
Every memory of your lips
Or your fingers
How they graze
The surface of my skin
And the way you say my name
No matter how I tried
I could never forget the girl
Who made Hell bearable

Till We Meet Again Someday

I'd wait an eternity for you
If that's what it took
Just to see you again
If only you understood
That you're the only love for me
No one else could even come close
No matter how far apart we drift
It's your love I'll be waiting for

Eternally yours

You are not alone
I am here with you
Holding your frail hands
In the dark
Always

This is not the end

THIS IS ME, BARE BONES AND SKIN FOR ALL TO SEE
THIS IS MY HEART ON PAPER
THE INK, MY BLOOD
HOW I FELT IN MY DARKEST TIMES
AND HOW I FOUGHT MY WAY OUT
SOME THINGS I'VE SEEN ALONG THE WAY
GOOD AND BAD
SOME THINGS I CAN'T STOP SEEING
UNTIL I WRITE THEM DOWN
TO FREE IT FROM MY HEAD

THE FOOL'S BOOK

Made in the USA
Middletown, DE
22 July 2022